D0513657

Aberdeenshire Libraries
www.aberdeenshire.gov.uk/libraries
Renewals Hotline 01224 661511
Downloads available from
www.aberdeenshirelibraries.lib.overdrive.com

- 3 APR 2015

13 MAY 2016
HQ

ABERDEENSHIRE
LIBRARY &
INFORMATION SERVICES

WITHDRAWN
FROM LIBRARY

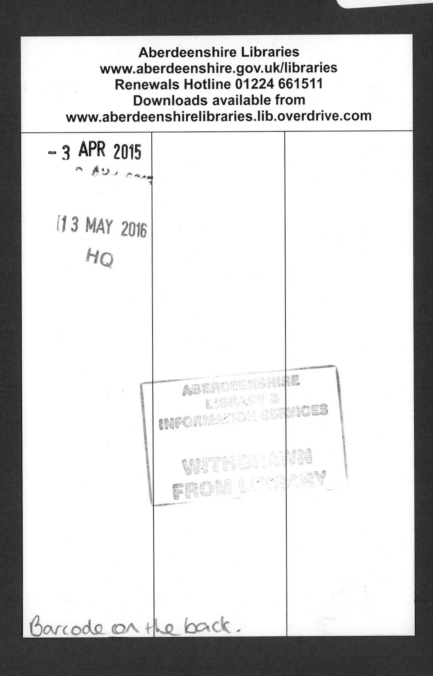

Barcode on the back.

ART AND CULTURE

Discover The Anglo-Saxons

ART AND CULTURE

Moira Butterfield

W

FRANKLIN WATTS
LONDON • SYDNEY

First published in 2014
by Franklin Watts

Copyright © Franklin Watts 2014

Franklin Watts
338 Euston Road
London, NW1 3BH

Franklin Watts Australia
Level 17/207 Kent Street
Sydney, NSW 2000

Editor in chief: John C. Miles
Series editor: Sarah Ridley
Art director: Peter Scoulding
Series designer: John Christopher/White Design
Picture researcher: Kathy Lockley

Dewey number: 941.01

Hardback ISBN 978 1 4451 3341 6
Library eBook ISBN 978 1 4451 3342 3

Printed in China

Franklin Watts is a division of Hachette Children's Books,
an Hachette UK company.

www.hachette.co.uk

Picture credits
The Art Archive/Alamy: 16-17; The Ashmolean Museum, Oxford/ The Art Archive:
22-23; Bridgeman Art Library/Getty Images: Title page, 18-19, 24; © The British
Library Board: 11, 27; The British Library/Robana via Getty Images: 10, 12, 14-15;
The British Library/Robana/TopFoto: 9; © The Trustees of the British Museum: 25;
CM Dixon/HIP/TopFoto: 20, 21; Ealdgyth: 23; Fine Art Images /Heritage Images/
Getty Images: 13; The Granger Collection/TopFoto: 7, 8; Courtesy Michael J King: 8;
INTERFOTO Alamy: 28-29; Museum of London/Heritage Images/Getty Images: 26;
Royal Library, Stockholm, Sweden / Bridgeman Art Library London: COVER;
© Colin Young/Dreamstime.com: 6

*Every attempt has been made to clear copyright. Should there be any inadvertent
omission please apply to the publisher for rectification.*

CONTENTS

MEET THE ANGLO-SAXONS

In the 400s CE new settlers arrived in southern Britain from Denmark, Germany and the Netherlands. We call them the Anglo-Saxons. We can discover a little about their lives through the art they left behind.

6

FINE CRAFTS

Anglo-Saxon men and women were craftspeople who made fine decorated weapons, jewellery and embroidery. Many surviving examples of Anglo-Saxon crafts come from excavated graves. Important nobles had expensive treasures buried with them. Ordinary people's graves contain less expensive objects.

Fine metalwork
A reconstruction of the helmet found in an Anglo-Saxon burial chamber at Sutton Hoo in Suffolk.

Lost treasures

The Anglo-Saxon period was an era of war. At different times, Vikings invaded from the north and Normans invaded from the south. Many manuscripts and beautiful objects of the time are likely to have been destroyed by the invaders.

FIRST WORDS

Early on in Anglo-Saxon times nobody wrote anything down. That changed from around 650 CE onwards, when Christianity reached England. Monasteries were set up by monks who came from abroad, bringing learning with them. In the monasteries young monks were taught to write and to illuminate (decorate) manuscripts. Religious works, poetry and written histories survive from these times, but the documents are very rare and precious.

ART FOR RULERS

The wealthiest people in Anglo-Saxon England were the noble rulers and their families, and important churchmen such as bishops. This rich group paid craftspeople to make the finest objects and commissioned beautifully decorated manuscripts.

Illuminated art

Created by monks in Northumbria, this illumination comes from a 700s CE copy of an even older Bible. It shows Ezra the scribe at work.

SPECIAL STORYTELLING

The Anglo-Saxons passed on their myths and history by reciting stories to each other in the form of long 'epic' poems that were easy to remember. A few of these tales were eventually written down.

We know that Anglo-Saxons valued music because minstrels were sometimes rewarded by their lords with jewels and even land. Some musical instruments and song lyrics have survived but we cannot tell for sure what the music of the time actually sounded like.

A FEAST OF STORIES

Anglo-Saxon rulers lived in large wooden halls with their warriors. In the evenings they feasted together and were entertained by storytellers called 'scops', and musicians called 'gleemen'. The storytellers knew a range of epic poems, telling of great battles or mythical warriors fighting monsters. Feuds, treachery, bravery and death were popular themes.

Lovely lyre
A reconstruction of an Anglo-Saxon lyre. Lyres were played at feasts.

IMAGINE THE HALL

It would have been atmospheric and exciting to listen to a well-told story in a hall hung with animal skins and lit by a crackling fire. The lord of the hall sat on his wooden throne and his warriors sat at benches, drinking mead and eating roast meats. Harpists or lyre-players played during the meal, and afterwards there might be jesters and singers. Then the storyteller stood, to the cheers of the warriors, and began his gripping tale. He may have occasionally played his own lyre to make the story sound even more dramatic.

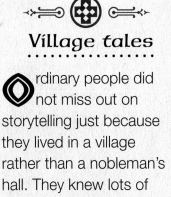

Village tales

Ordinary people did not miss out on storytelling just because they lived in a village rather than a nobleman's hall. They knew lots of tales themselves, and sometimes a travelling storyteller visited, entertaining people in return for some food, shelter and payment.

9

Happy hall

This scene from an Anglo-Saxon calendar shows nobles at a feast. Wine is being poured into a drinking horn by a man on the left of the picture.

HEROES AND MONSTERS

*B*eowulf is the most famous story that survives from Anglo-Saxon times. It was passed on by word-of-mouth for generations before it was finally written down some time in the 1000s.

English long ago

*B*eowulf was written in Old English, the language of Anglo-Saxon England. It needs translating for modern English speakers to understand. Here is the original beginning of *Beowulf* and a modern translation by the Irish poet Seamus Heaney:

Hwæt! We Gar-Dena in gear-dagum
þeod-cyninga, þrym gefrunon,
hu ða æþelingas ellen fremedo.

So. The Spear-Danes in days gone by,
And the Kings who ruled them had
courage and greatness.

Beowulf manuscript
The British Library has the only surviving manuscript of *Beowulf*, created about 1,000 years ago.

Battling beasts
Anglo-Saxons believed in mythical monsters, such as this two-headed snake, which appears in the *Beowulf* manuscript (see left).

A POETRY ADVENTURE

Beowulf is an action-packed tale of a brave warrior-leader called Beowulf, who fights evil monsters. It is an epic poem of around 3,000 lines in length, and it is exciting, scary and violent. Around a thousand years after it was first written down, it inspired Anglo-Saxon scholar J.R.R. Tolkien to write *The Lord of the Rings*, which also has heroes fighting dangerous monsters.

A HERO DIES

In the poem, a man-eating monster called Grendel terrorises a Danish kingdom. The king asks Beowulf and his men to help, and Beowulf kills first Grendel, then Grendel's monstrous and murderous mother. Beowulf eventually becomes king himself but he has to fight a dragon who goes on the rampage after someone steals from its treasure hoard. Beowulf kills the dragon but dies himself, a hero to the end.

Wondrous words

Beowulf is rhythmic, like a chant, but it doesn't rhyme. Instead it uses lots of assonance – when the same vowel sounds are repeated in the same sentence. It also uses alliteration – when words in the same sentence start with the same letter. Spot two Ss (alliteration) and two 'ou' sounds (assonance) in this translated line about the dragon (called the mound-keeper) that Beowulf killed.

The mound-keeper went into a spasm and spouted deadly flames when it felt the stroke.

11

THE FIRST BOOKS

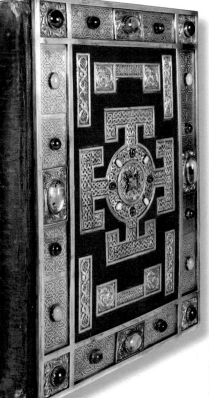

When the Anglo-Saxons first arrived in England they were pagan, but in the 600s monks came from other parts of Europe to convert them to Christianity. The visitors set up monasteries where the first books ever made in England were created.

Lindisfarne Gospels
One monk, called Aldred, created the *Lindisfarne Gospels* in around 700. By hand he wrote out the four gospels of the Bible and illustrated them.

Inside art
The first page of St Matthew's Gospel in the *Lindisfarne Gospels.*

Colourful art

Illuminated manuscripts are the only illustrated art we have left from the time. We can tell from them that the artists liked to use bright dramatic-looking colours such as deep red, emerald green, golden yellow and vivid blue.

MANUSCRIPTS AND MONKS
The monks who arrived from Europe brought decorated manuscripts with them and taught Anglo-Saxon monks to copy the style. They hand-wrote in Latin on animal skin parchment and illustrated their documents with illuminations – tiny pictures and patterns finished off with gold and silver. The books they created were mainly religious, but they also wrote history books and poetry. Wealthy nobles paid for books to be written for them and these books were given fine covers of gold and silver, studded with gemstones.

ILLUMINATING TOOLS

To make parchment, animal skin was soaked, scraped, stretched and cleaned until it was smooth and dry. Inks for the pictures were made from ground-up rocks, plants and animals. For instance, purple ink, used in the most expensive books, came from shellfish. Pens were cut from birds' flight feathers and inkwells were made from animal horn.

Perfect patterns

The Anglo-Saxon illuminators loved adding intricate swirling patterns that wound around their illustrations and letters. It's a style that was used in jewellery and metalwork, too.

AUTHORS AND IDEAS

We know very little about the people who wrote the Anglo-Saxon manuscripts that survive to this day, but we can tell something about what they thought by looking at their work.

HOLY WRITERS

The Anglo-Saxon history we have was written down by two monks – Gildas, who lived in the 500s, and Bede, who lived in the 700s. We cannot say for sure what is true and what is legend in the stories they tell of ancient kings and battles, but we know that they saw the world from a religious viewpoint. For instance, Gildas called his history *The Ruin of Britain* and thought that God sent wars as a punishment for the sins of local kings and churchmen. Anglo-Saxon poetry was religious, too. The earliest English poem that we know of is a nine-line hymn probably written in the 600s by a monk called Caedmon.

An old idea made new

Caedmon's nine-line hymn, the earliest English poem in existence, includes the word *middingard*, which will be recognisable to *The Lord of the Rings* fans. It means 'middle earth', the land of humans as opposed to Heaven or Hell.

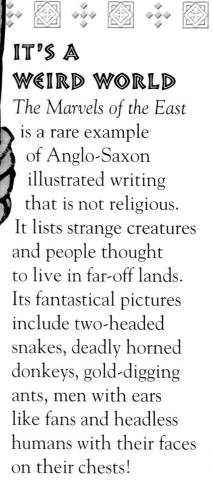

IT'S A WEIRD WORLD

The Marvels of the East is a rare example of Anglo-Saxon illustrated writing that is not religious. It lists strange creatures and people thought to live in far-off lands. Its fantastical pictures include two-headed snakes, deadly horned donkeys, gold-digging ants, men with ears like fans and headless humans with their faces on their chests!

15

Monster man
A blemmya, a giant man with his face on his chest, is one illustration from *The Marvels of the East*.

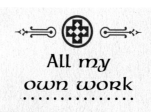

All my own work

A writer called Cynewulf was the first English author that we know of to write his own name on his work. He interwove symbols representing the letters of his name into the manuscripts of his poems.

eibi draconef longuidinem
d. pedi iaftrii finecolunarii

RIDDLE OF THE BOX

Anglo-Saxons loved riddles as well as epic adventure poems. One of the most beautifully-made objects to survive from these far-off times has a riddle carved into it.

✤═◆═✤ Words we know
. . . .

We still use versions of Old English words, including days of the week:

Monday: *Monandæg*
(the day of the moon);

Tuesday: *Tiwesdæg*
(the day of the god *Tiw*);

Wednesday: *Wodnesdæg*
(the day of the god *Woden*);

Thursday: *Þunresdæg*
(the day of the god *Thunor*);

Friday: *Frigedæg*
(the day of the goddess *Friga*);

Saturday: *Sæternesdæg*
(the day of the Roman god Saturn);

Sunday: *Sunnandæg*
(the day of the sun).

Casket of questions
One end of the Franks Casket. The carvings on this part of the casket show the story of Romulus and Remus. The words are written in an ancient alphabet called 'runic'.

CLEVER CASKET
The Franks Casket was made around 700. It is carved with a mixture of pictures and words, including an Old English riddle that translates as:

The fish beat up the seas on to the mountainous cliff. The King of terror became sad when he swam onto the shingle.

The riddle's answer is 'whale bone'. The casket is made from the bone of a beached whale.

RIDDLE OF THE MAKERS

The words on the casket are written in an Old English dialect (a local version of the language) that comes from Northumbria in northern England. We don't know who made it, but it seems they had religious knowledge, so perhaps they worked in a Northumbrian monastery. Whoever did it carved a picture of the wise men visiting the newborn Jesus but also showed an ancient Roman emperor invading Jerusalem and some scenes from mysterious pagan legends.

◆◈◆ Have you heard this one?

Anglo-Saxon riddles were jokey and sometimes very rude! People recited them to entertain their friends. Here is a translation of a simple one to try yourself:

On the way a miracle.
Water becomes bone.

The answer is – ice!

MASTERS
OF METAL

Anglo-Saxon metalworkers were famous across Europe for their talent. We know very little about them, only that they made some fabulous objects.

BURIED TREASURES

Anglo-Saxon goldsmiths specialised in decoration we call cloisonné. They placed tiny pieces of glass or coloured stones into gold, making complicated and beautiful patterns. Examples of their astonishing skill have been found in graves or as part of buried treasure hoards such as the Staffordshire Hoard – over 1,500 fragments found on farmland in 2009. The finest pieces of all came from the burial of an Anglo-Saxon king at Sutton Hoo, Suffolk.

In demand

Anglo-Saxon goldsmiths made lots of objects for churches, such as altar plates and relic boxes. They even travelled to Rome to work for the Pope.

SPARROWHAWK THE GOLDSMITH

We know of one goldsmith, called Spearhafoc (Old English for 'sparrowhawk'). He was a monk who lived in the 1000s, and he got promoted in the Church because of his marvellous metalwork skills. However, when he failed to get the job of Bishop of London he vanished, taking with him all the gold and jewels he had been given to make a crown for King Edward the Confessor. Nobody ever caught up with him, it seems!

Brilliant brooch

A brooch made from gold, garnets (the red pieces inlaid between the gold) and shell. It was found in an Anglo-Saxon grave.

Saint Dunstan and the Devil

A famous Anglo-Saxon churchman called Dunstan was a skilled metalworker who eventually became a saint. Legend has it that he once grabbed the Devil's nose with his red-hot metalworking tongs.

BEASTLY ART

Anglo-Saxon artists used lots of animals to decorate their manuscripts, metalwork and carvings. They often wound creatures around each other to create complicated patterns.

Fantastic ornament
This intricately worked ornament with its amazing detail is from the Sutton Hoo burial in Suffolk.

Old style
When Anglo-Saxon monks drew pagan mythical animals on their religious manuscripts, they were carrying on an old traditional style of art. They did not carry on the old pagan beliefs, though.

MAGICAL MEANINGS
In pagan Anglo-Saxon times animals had symbolic meanings. Snakes with wolf-like heads might have represented protection from harm. Wolves, boars and birds of prey may have represented power and victory. It's possible that people may have thought that animal strengths might magically transfer to the objects they decorated, such as helmets and swords. In the poem *Beowulf* (see p10) a smith makes a weapon and decorates it with boars' heads so it will become magically strong.

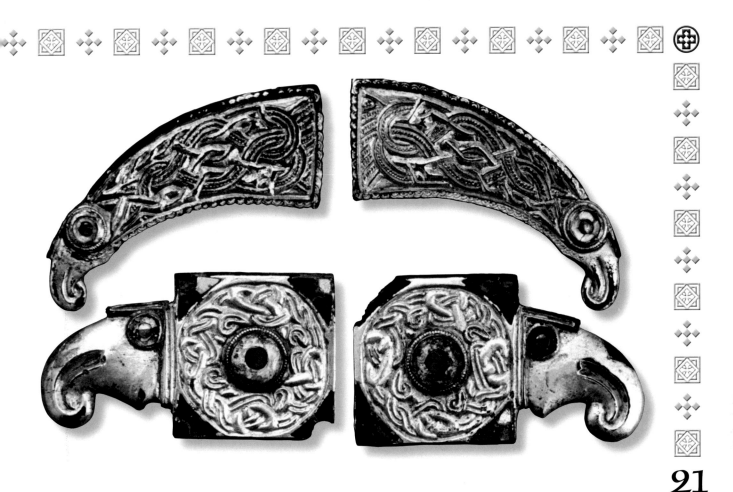

Birds' heads

The pair of bronze birds at the top were found in an Anglo-Saxon grave at Taplow, Buckinghamshire. Look for the use of geometric design. The lower pair of birds' heads once decorated a lyre at Sutton Hoo in Suffolk.

ART OF THE GODS

Pagan Anglo-Saxons worshipped gods and goddesses who had their own magical animal helpers. For instance, the god Woden had wolves and ravens as his helpers, and he could turn into strange creatures unknown to humans. It's possible that pagans put legendary animals in their art to create some kind of magical connection to their gods, but we cannot know for sure. When belief in Christianity took over in England, the ancient meanings of the pagan animal symbols were lost or changed.

Animals for the elite

Expensive objects for wealthy people, including drinking horns, musical instruments and fine battlegear, were often decorated with symbols of fierce hunting animals, such as wolves and birds of prey. They probably showed that the person owning them was powerful and important.

WHO MADE THAT?

We know hardly any names of Anglo-Saxon craftspeople, but we can learn about their work by studying the pieces they made and by experimenting to see how they did it.

HOW WAS IT DONE?

There are very few descriptions of Anglo-Saxon craftspeople doing their work, so archaeologists must do practical experiments to try to discover their secrets. For instance, by making glass for themselves, they have discovered some of the minerals that Anglo-Saxon glassmakers added to their glass. The blue colour of the bowl on the right was made by adding copper to the molten glass.

First recyclers

The Anglo-Saxon glassmakers were early recyclers. We know that they often melted down old glass for reuse. They even melted and reused bits of ancient Roman glass from mosaics.

SEE THE SKILL

Anglo-Saxon craftspeople had great skill, which can be seen by looking closely at the pieces they made. This beautiful blue drinking cup, the Cuddesdon Bowl, was found in the grave of a nobleman buried during the 600s. It was probably intended for him to use in the afterlife. Try to imagine it being made in the heat of a glassmaker's workshop. The person who made it blew the glass into shape and then dribbled hot liquid glass onto it to make swirls and loops. The Anglo-Saxon glassmakers were also experts at making glass beads with complicated coloured layers, stripes and dots. Lead oxide was sometimes added to make the beads sparkle.

Blue bowl
The Cuddesdon Bowl, found in the grave of a nobleman in Oxfordshire, dates from around 600. It measures 11.5cm across.

Sacred glass

A very delicate glass bowl, called the Shaftesbury Bowl, was discovered in front of the high altar of Shaftesbury Abbey. It is the only piece of late Anglo-Saxon glass in existence, and it's thought possible that it may have once held the heart of King Canute, who died in Shaftesbury in 1035.

MADE FOR THE TOP

The Alfred Jewel and the Fuller Brooch are both examples of very finely-made objects that were probably created for a king. One of these fine pieces may hold the answer to a mystery.

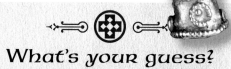

24

THE KING'S POINTER

In 1693 the Alfred Jewel was dug up in a field in Somerset. It contains a small enamelled picture protected by a piece of clear quartz crystal, surrounded by delicate goldwork. Writing round the outside translates as: *Alfred had me made.* King Alfred, ruler of Wessex in southern England, may have had it made in the 800s. It is thought to be the top part of an aestel, a rod used for pointing at the words in a book, perhaps a large religious one being read out loud in a monastery.

Alfred Jewel

Who is the mystery figure shown in the Alfred Jewel? Do you think it looks like the staring figure on the far right?

What's your guess?

Curling leaves are carved on the back of the Alfred Jewel, and at the bottom there is a dragon-like head where the pointer would have fitted. Nobody knows for sure what these symbols might represent. Could the leaves be the Tree of Life, perhaps? It's all guesswork!

Secrets of the brooch

In the centre of the Fuller Brooch the figure representing *Taste* has a hand in his mouth. *Smell* stands with his hands behind his back between two plants. *Hearing* cups his ear with his hand and *Touch* rubs his hands together. Around the outside humans, animals and plants might represent different aspects of the creation story.

IS SIGHT THE SECRET?

The Fuller Brooch was made in the late 800s using beaten silver. It may even have been made in King Alfred's court workshop, though nobody knows for sure. It is decorated with figures representing the five senses. The figure in the centre has large staring eyes and holds two branches. It represents the sense of sight, and some scholars think that the figure on the Alfred Jewel (left) could be the same symbol.

Fuller Brooch
Possibly made in King Alfred's court workshops, this brooch of hammered silver is in excellent condition.

IN FASHION

Anglo-Saxons liked to have objects decorated in the latest style, just as people do today. Recognising the styles helps archaeologists to date the pieces.

Brooch
A square-headed brooch, worn by fashionable Anglo-Saxon women.

No more buried treasure

When the Anglo-Saxons became Christian, they were no longer buried with objects to take to a pagan afterlife, so we have far fewer examples of the things they owned.

PAGAN PATTERNS

In early Anglo-Saxon times, when people were still pagan, they were generally buried with objects that were decorated with strange creatures and geometric patterns (see p20). They seemed to like styles of jewellery similar to fashions found in pagan Scandinavia and Germany. For instance, in early graves, women were sometimes buried with square-headed brooches that were also fashionable in Scandinavia. They used the brooches to fasten their clothing.

SWIRLY STYLE

In the late 800s King Alfred made Winchester his capital and it became an important centre of manuscript illumination. Between 966 and 1066 the manuscripts and objects made in this area had a particular type of swirly decoration, which is now called the 'Winchester School'. It used plenty of acanthus leaves and tendrils twining around birds and animals (an acanthus is a type of plant with curly leaves). Everyday objects had this decoration as well as manuscripts, so it must have been the local fashion.

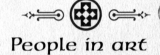

People in art

Once the Anglo-Saxons became Christian they began to depict more figures in their art, showing Bible stories and saints. The artists of the Winchester School liked to give their figures swirling clothes of rich colours.

Border of leaves

A page from *The Benedictional of Saint Aethelwold*, created at Winchester during the 900s. It shows Jesus entering Jerusalem. Look for the acanthus leaves in the decorated border.

STITCHING ART

Anglo-Saxon women did their own weaving and sewing at home, and some were employed to create stunning embroidery that was prized throughout Europe as a fine art.

EMBROIDERY TO ORDER

Skilled embroiderers were commissioned to decorate vestments – robes worn by important churchmen such as bishops. Luxury gold and silver threads were used to sew amazingly detailed pictures such as animals, foliage and patterns that looked like the illumination found on religious manuscripts (see p27). Much of this wonderful embroidery has now been lost and we only know how fine it was from writings of the time. We have just a few rare examples, found in the graves of Anglo-Saxon bishops buried in their robes.

(see p27)

28

Gone for gold
....

It is thought that a lot of fine Anglo-Saxon embroidery has been deliberately destroyed over the years, to get the valuable gold that was sewn into it as thread.

SEWING HISTORY

In 1066 Duke William of Normandy invaded England and brought to an end Anglo-Saxon rule. His victory was commemorated in one of the world's most famous embroideries – the Bayeux Tapestry. It is possible that it was made by English needleworkers, though we don't know for sure. Whoever sewed it used coloured wools on pieces of linen, following a cartoon design drawn by artists. It was sewn by a number of expert embroiderers and their panels were then joined together to make a work nearly 70m long.

The last battle

The Bayeux Tapestry shows the Anglo-Saxons being defeated by the invading Normans at the Battle of Hastings.

Nearly a wrap

In the late 1700s the Bayeux Tapestry was very nearly destroyed. It was about to be used as scrap fabric and wrapped over the cargo in a wagon to protect it from the rain. Luckily it was saved at the last minute.

GLOSSARY

Afterlife Belief in a life after death.

Alliteration When words in the same sentence start with the same letter.

Anglo-Saxons Settlers who arrived in southern Britain in the 400s CE, from the areas we now call Denmark, Germany and the Netherlands.

Assonance When the same vowel sounds are repeated in the same sentence of a poem.

Benedictional A book containing a collection of benedictions, or blessings, used during services held by the Roman Catholic Church.

Christianity Belief in the God of the Holy Bible.

Cloisonné A method of inlaying tiny pieces of coloured glass or stone into gold to make patterns.

Commission When somebody is paid to create something for someone, perhaps a piece of jewellery or embroidery.

Dialect A local version of a language.

Elite The most important and wealthiest people in society.

Epic poem A long story written in a series of short lines.

Foliage Plant leaves, often used in Anglo-Saxon designs.

Geometric A pattern made up of regular shapes and lines.

Gleemen Anglo-Saxon musicians who played at feasts.

Hoard A collection of valuable objects buried in the ground.

Illumination Decoration painted onto a manuscript.

Inlay To decorate an object by laying pieces of another material into it.

Lyre A musical instrument with strings.

Manuscript A handwritten document.

Mead An alcoholic drink made from fermented honey.

ANGLO-SAXON TIMELINE

410 CE The Roman army leaves Britain. In the years that follow local warlords take control of different areas.

449 Angles and Saxons arrive by boat in south-east Britain. The Britons fight to push them back.

540 The invading Angles, Saxons and Jutes conquer England.

563 Irish monk Columba founds a Christian monastery on the island of Iona.

585 By now seven separate kingdoms have formed in England – Mercia, East Anglia, Northumberland, Essex, Wessex, Sussex and Kent. Each has their own king. Over time, some kings become *bretwalda* – overlords of the other kings.

597 Aethelberht, King of Kent, becomes the first Anglo-Saxon Christian leader, converted by the monk Augustine. Gradually others convert to Christianity.

620 (approx) The death and burial of East Anglian King Redwald at Sutton Hoo in Suffolk.

664 A meeting at Whitby decides between Celtic Christianity and the Christianity of Rome. The Christianity of Rome is preferred.

731 A monk called Bede finishes writing a history of Britain, the best source of history we have about this time.

789 The first recorded Viking attack on the British Isles, at Portland in Dorset.

793 Vikings attack the monastery at Lindisfarne.

865 A big Viking force, the Great Heathen Army, arrives and rampages across the country for the next 14 years.

Middingard Middle Earth, the land of humans as opposed to Heaven or Hell.

Old English The name we give to the language written and spoken by the Anglo-Saxons.

Paganism Belief in many gods and goddesses.

Parchment Animal skin prepared so it can be used for writing.

Relic The remains of a saint or an object associated with the Bible.

Sacred Something that is believed to be connected magically to God.

Scop An Anglo-Saxon storyteller who performed at events, such as feasts.

Symbolic Something that represents a hidden meaning.

Vestments Robes worn by important churchmen such as bishops.

Wessex An important Anglo-Saxon kingdom in southern and western England.

Winchester School A style of Anglo-Saxon art in the late 900s, with lots of swirling plants twined around animals and birds.

Woden An important god in pagan Anglo-Saxon times.

WEBLINKS

Here are some websites with information about Anglo-Saxon art and stories.

http://www.youtube.com/watch?v=AaB0trCztM0
Hear poet Seamus Heaney read his wonderful 1999 translation of *Beowulf*.

http://www.wearmouth-jarrow.org.uk/story/creators
See Anglo-Saxon monk-craftsmen at work in 3D.

http://www.staffordshirehoard.org.uk/
Discover a hoard of Anglo-Saxon gold treasure.

http://www.bl.uk/onlinegallery/virtualbooks/index.html
Turn the pages of the beautiful Anglo-Saxon *Lindisfarne Gospels*.

878 Alfred, King of Wessex, defeats a Danish Viking force at the Battle of Edington, to save his kingdom. The Danes and the Anglo-Saxons agree to the Treaty of Wedmore, that split England between them.

899 Alfred dies. He is succeeded as King of Wessex by his son, Edward.

911 Alfred's daughter Aethelflaed rules over Mercia after the death of her husband.

937 Athelstan, King of Wessex and Mercia, defeats an army of Vikings and Scots at the Battle of Brunanburh. He then rules over England.

1016 Danish King Cnut becomes King of England, deposing Ethelred the Unready. Anglo-Danish kings rule England for a while.

1042 Edward, son of Ethelred the Unready, takes power. Brought up in Normandy, he apparently promised his throne to his great-nephew, William, when he died.

1066 Harold Godwinson is chosen as king but reigns for only ten months. The Anglo-Saxons are defeated by William, Duke of Normandy, at the Battle of Hastings.

31

INDEX